OPAL PIPES AND BELEMNITES
AGE: 100 million years.
LOCATION: Disused mineshaft, Coober Pedy, Australia.
ARROWHEADS AND SPEARPOINTS
Flint. Obsidian. Chert.
LOCATION: Wyoming, USA.
COPROLITE
Fossilised dung from a large marine reptile.
LOCATION: Carnarvon Basin, Australia.
FULGURITE:PETRIFIED LIGHTNING
Formed in a flash when lightning strikes and melts the sand.
LOCATION: Sahara Desert, Algeria.
ZEBRA STONE AND ASTRONOMITE
A 600-million-year-old mystery.
LOCATION: East Kimberley, Australia.
IRON METEORITE
Shrapnel from a stray asteroid.
AGE: 4.5 billion years.
LOCATION: Campo del Cielo, Argentina.
FOSSIL TEETH AND FOSSIL BONES
Geological evidence of evolution and extinction, survival and diversity.
LOCATION: Morocco.

*In memory of Pat Quilty*

First published in 2019
by Walker Books Australia Pty Ltd
Locked Bag 22, Newtown
NSW 2042 Australia
www.walkerbooks.com.au

A catalogue record for this book is available from the National Library of Australia

ISBN: 978 1 76065 087 2

The illustrations for this book were created with mixed media on paper.
Typeset in Linden. Handlettered type by Walker Books, based on AquilineTwo.
Printed and bound in China

10 9 8 7 6 5 4 3 2 1

# THE BOOK OF STONE

MARK GREENWOOD • CORAL TULLOCH

It begins one stone at a time –

reaching down
turning pebbles over
searching for a story stone.

A stone is nature's gift
banded by swirls
shapes and colours
pits and patterns
polished smooth by time.

Some stones are cooked
in a bubbling soup
deep in the planet's core
poured molten upon the earth
cooled by the wind
on superstitious mountains.

A stone can be extraterrestrial –
a shooting star
a stray asteroid
a meteorite from Mars or beyond.

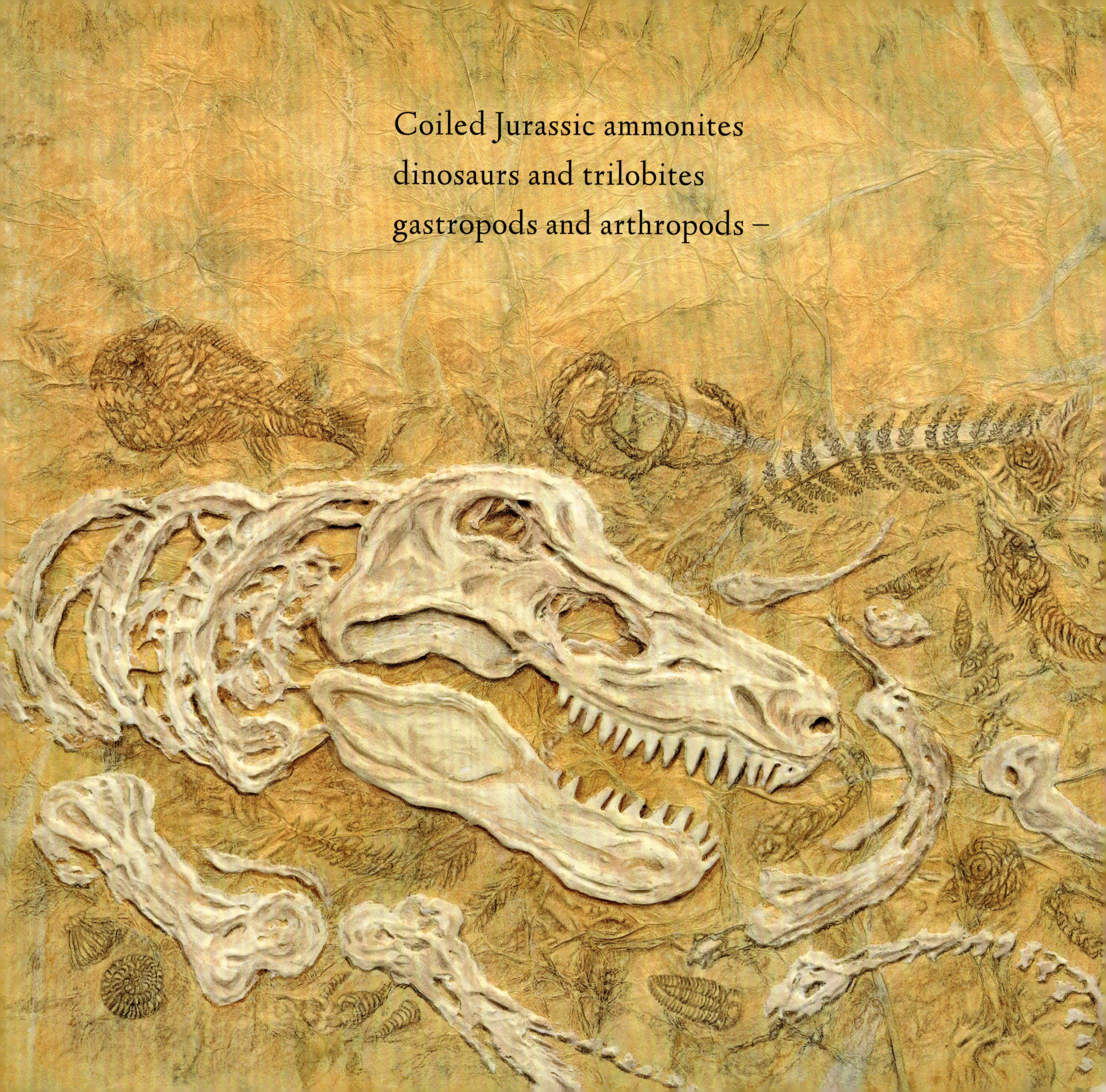

Coiled Jurassic ammonites
dinosaurs and trilobites
gastropods and arthropods –

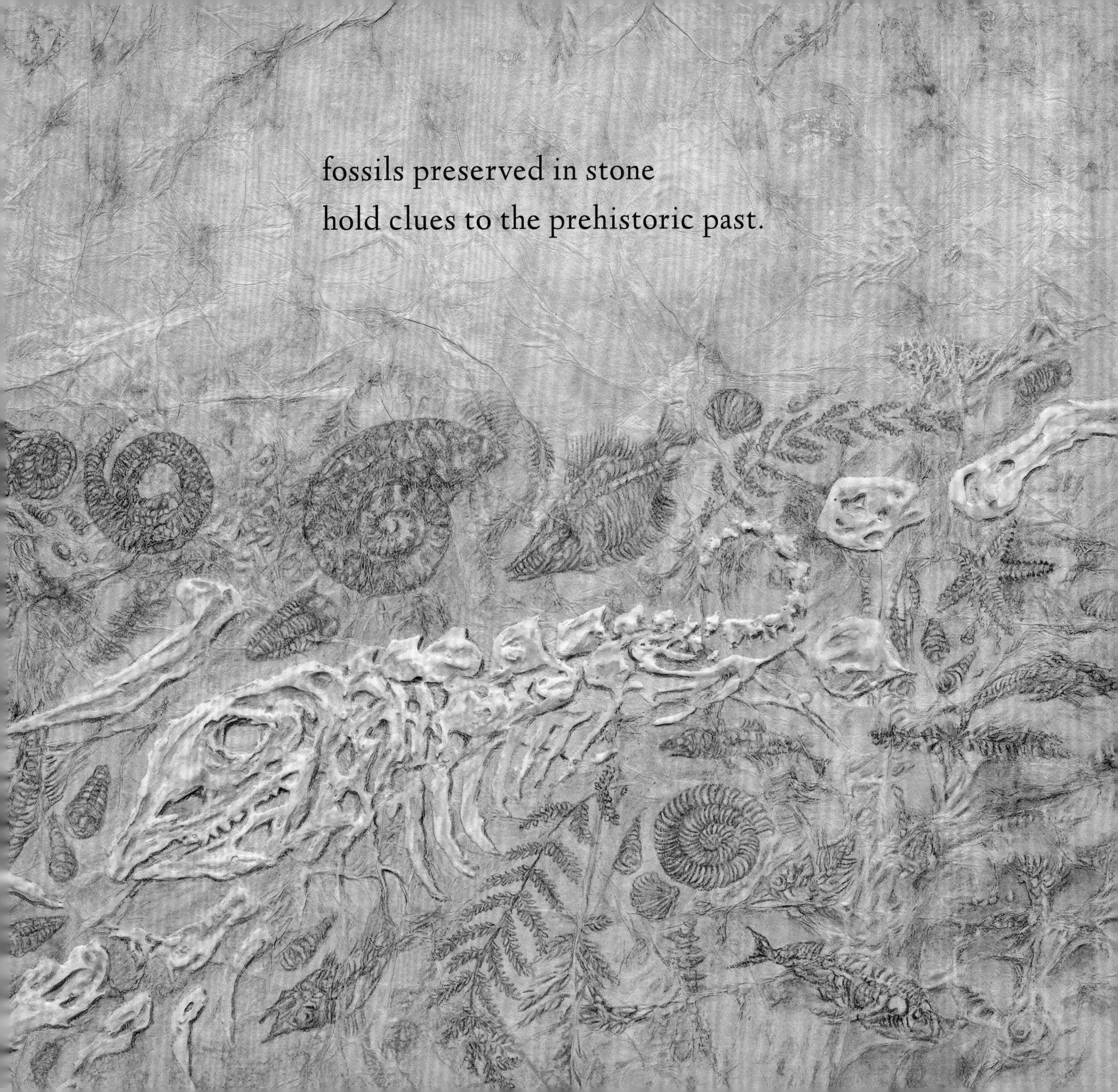

fossils preserved in stone
hold clues to the prehistoric past.

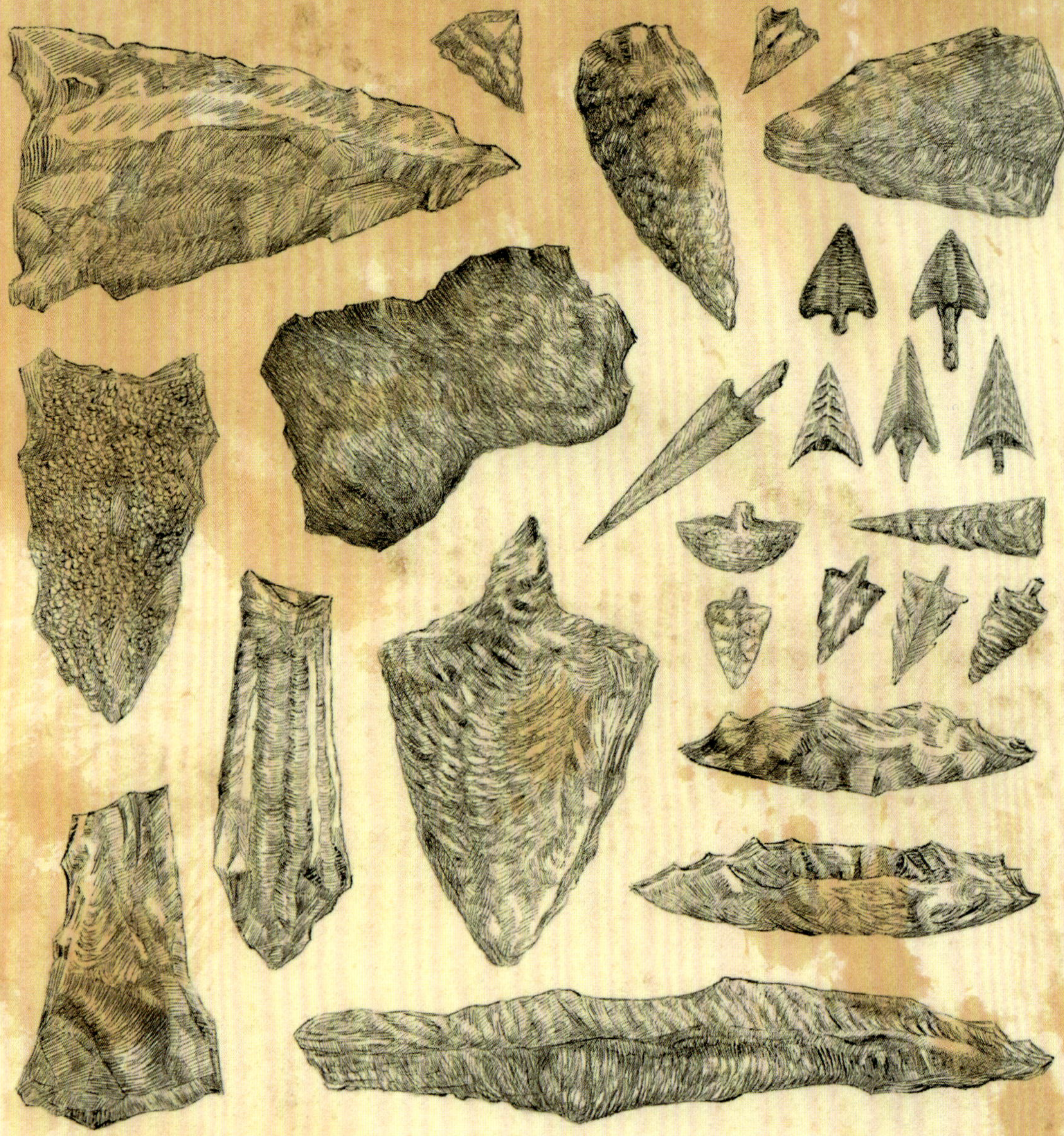

Stone is a tool of evolution –
axes and arrowheads

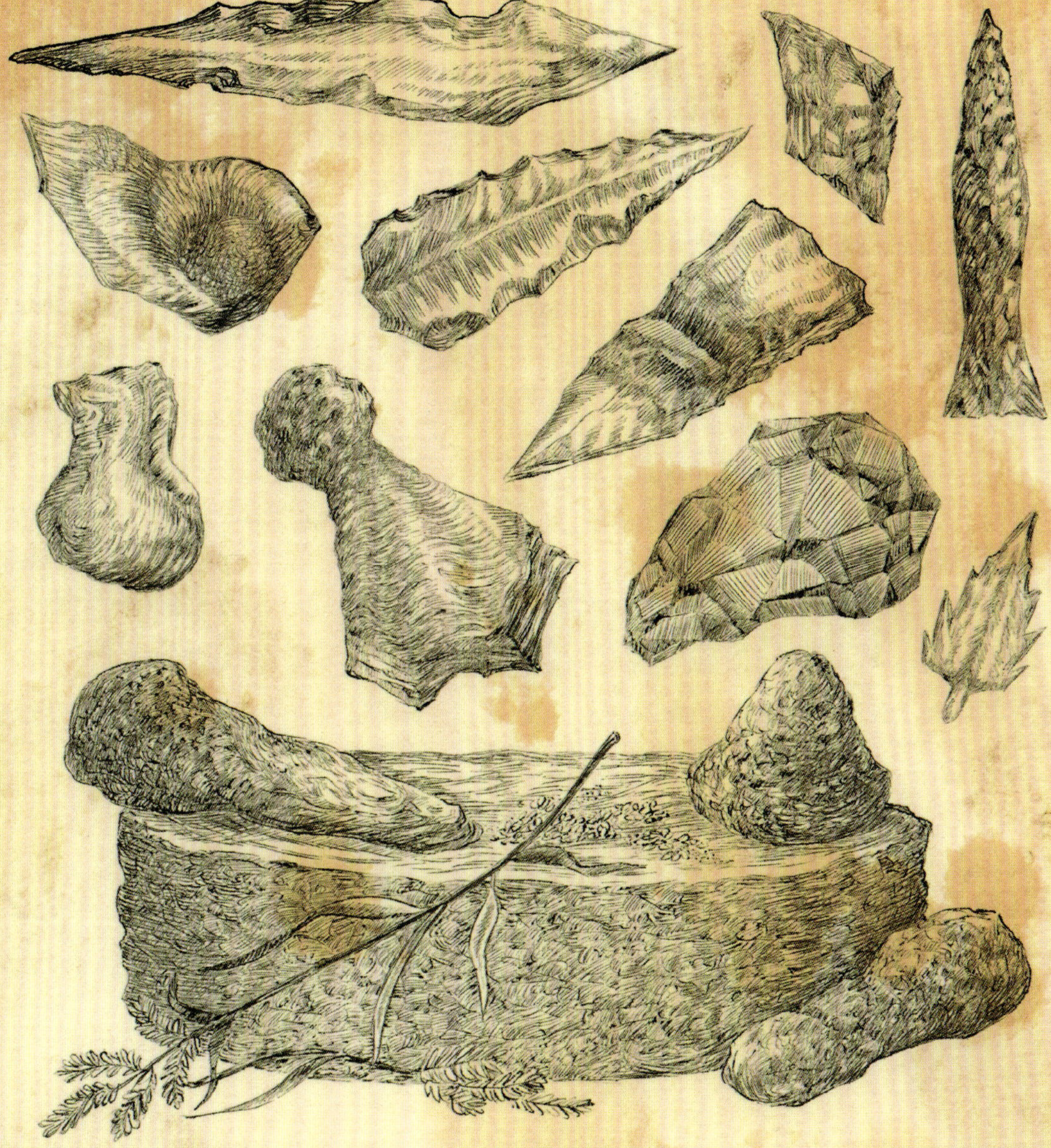

flint stones for fire
grinding stones for daily bread.

A stone is a rare treasure
buried in sediments of mud
a gem in the gravel of an ancient river
a glint in the chamber of a secret cave.

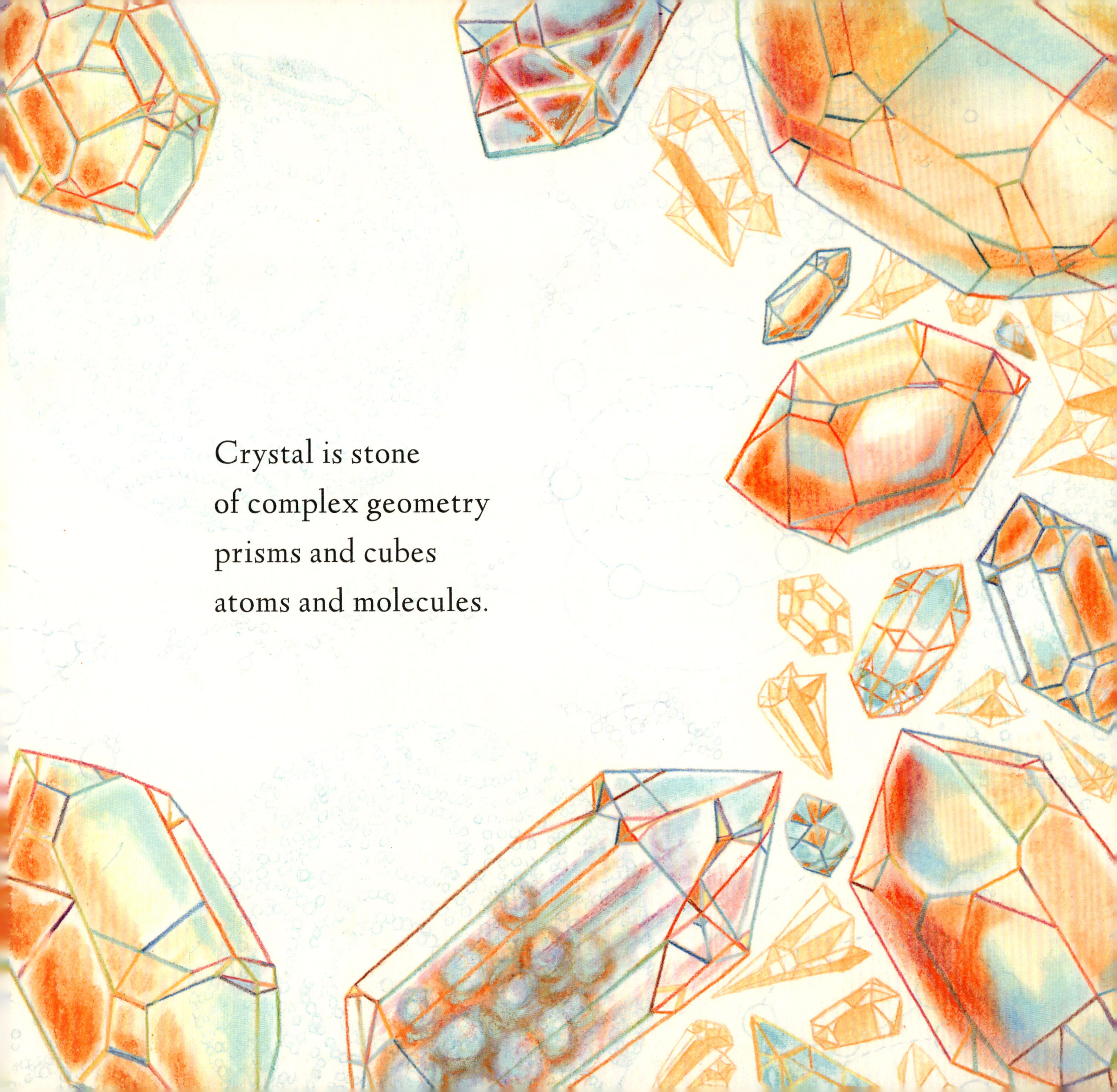

Crystal is stone
of complex geometry
prisms and cubes
atoms and molecules.

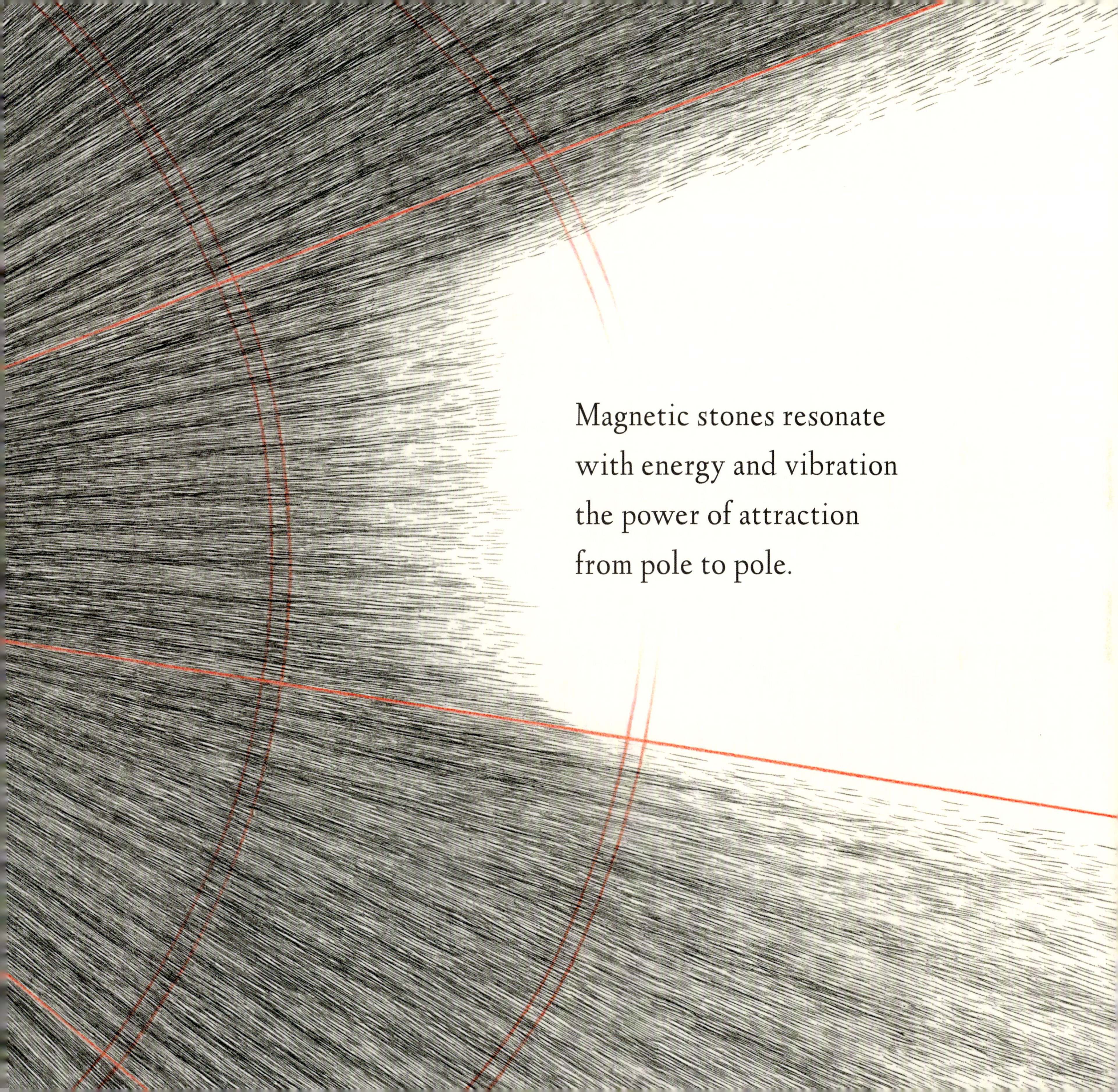

Magnetic stones resonate
with energy and vibration
the power of attraction
from pole to pole.

A stone is a talisman, an amulet, a lucky charm –

wishing stones and worry stones

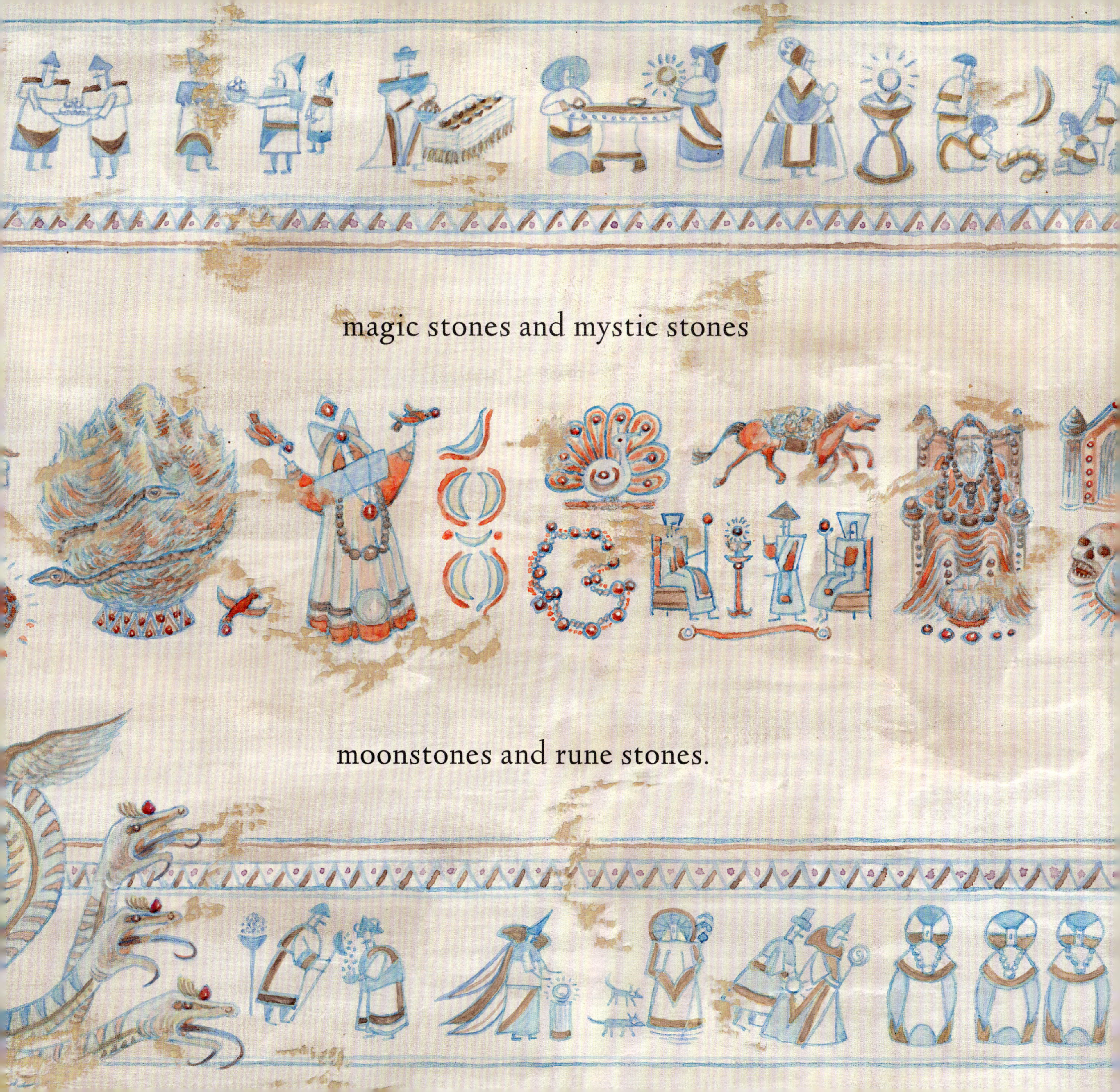

magic stones and mystic stones

moonstones and rune stones.

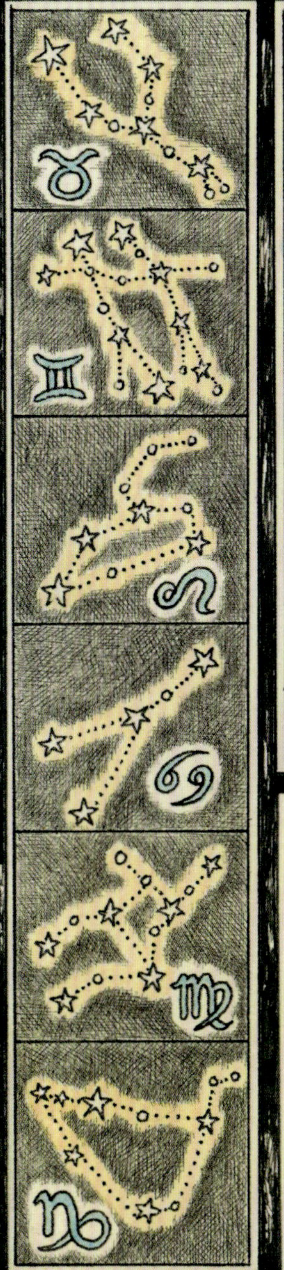

Astrology and astronomy –
the curious lore of constellations
twelve stones for each sign of the zodiac
a birthstone for each month of the year.

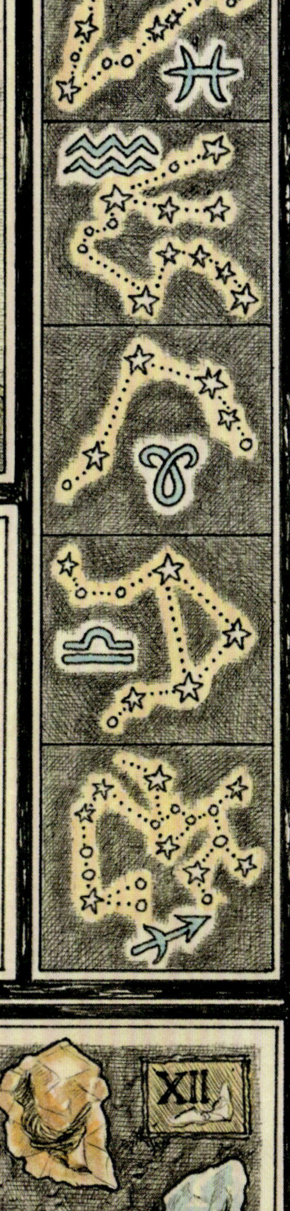

From stone
miracles and marvels
are made –

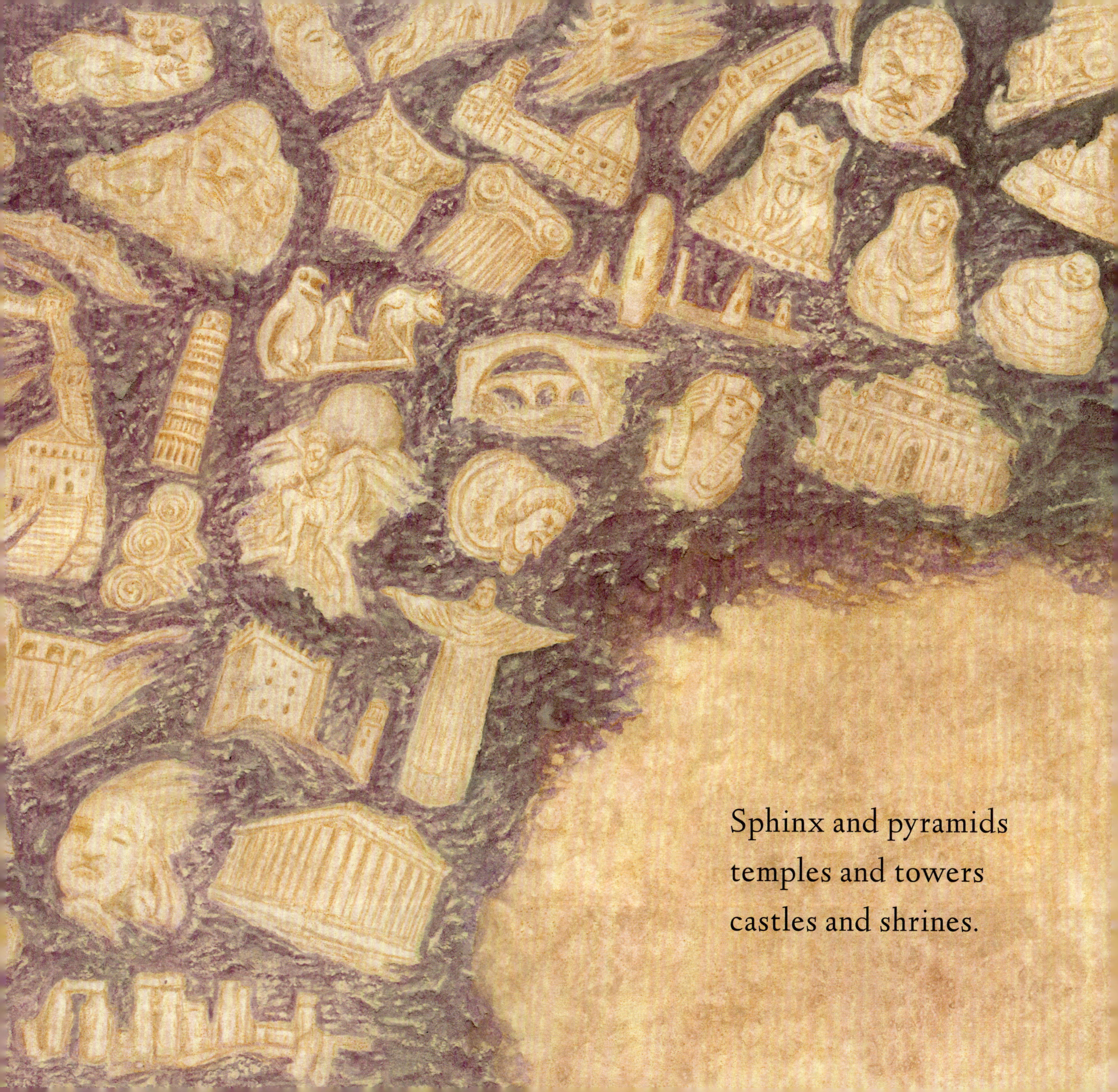

Sphinx and pyramids
temples and towers
castles and shrines.

Holy stones and altar stones –
a stone is a tomb
'graved with a sacred echo
of a life lived and loved.

PACE

Skipping stone.

Stepping stone.

A stone is a ripple of remembrance.

Every stone has a story –
an echo of time
the memory of a place
where wonder is found.

It begins one stone at a time.

LUCKY CHARM MAGNETITE
A magnetic stone, favoured by mystics to attract power and repel enchantments.
FOSSILISED FUNGIA
Coral turned to stone sheds light on Earth's past and holds clues to the future.
QUARTZ CRYSTALS
The mystery of symmetry and repetition, crystal faces and occlusions, phantoms and rainbows.
CRAZY LACE AGATE
Story stones pulsing with thermal patterns, coded by chemistry, laced with colours, shapes and swirls.
TRILOBITE (CALYMENE CELEBRA)
Ancient people wore trilobite amulets, believing the extinct arthropod harboured charms and powers.